Love Letters

(A collection of exciting, thrilling & interesting letters)

By

Abul Hashem

Ramesh Publishing House

New Delhi

Published by:
O.P. Gupta
for Ramesh Publishing House
Admin. Office: 12-H, New Daryaganj Road,
Opp. Traffic Kotwali, New Delhi-110002
✆ 23275124, 23275224
Telefax: 011-23275124
EMail: info@rameshpublishinghouse.com
Website: www.rameshpublishinghouse.com
Showroom: • 4457, Nai Sarak, Delhi-6 ✆ 23918938, 23918532
• 2604/16, Balaji Market, Nai Sarak, Delhi-6 ✆ 23253720

21st Edition: January, 2010

ISBN 81-86224-52-1

R-236

Price: Rs 35/- only

Printed at:
Giriraj Printer
Delhi

CONTENTS

1. *Love letter from an industrial tycoon to his Private Secretary*

(Full address of the writer, and date)

My dearest Pushpa,

I am sure you will be totally surprised to receive this letter.

I have been thinking of writing to you for over a month but I could not muster enough courage to do so, in spite of my best efforts. I am your employer. Speaking strictly in terms of office discipline and decorum, I should not express my love for you. It is below my dignity to fall in love with my own employee. But the sheer intensity of my most passionate love for you has forced me to throw all the existing barriers between you and me to the winds.

Pushpa, you have to blame your stunning beauty, which has aroused strange thoughts and sentiments in me all these days. When you, in order to take dictation, sit before me satisfying the thirst of my hungry eyes, and when your lovely, blue sparkling and big eyes rise up after every sentence to get locked up with my eyes, my emotions cannot remain dead or dull. Do you understand what I mean?

My tender heart is replete with (full of) pure and true love for you. Nobody in this world will be able to describe the depth and intensity of my love. The more I try to stop thinking about you. the more you come into my mind with all your grace, charm and beauty. Even as I pen (write) this letter, I feel as if your splendid figure is floating in front of my eyes. I always avail myself of every opportunity to have a look at your rosy cheeks, pink lips, long and pointed nose, slender fingers and your attractive figure. Today my boundless love for you is erupting through the medium of this epistle (letter). Honestly speaking, I am totally tired of the stolen glimpses of some of the captivating parts of your body.

It is for the first time that my heart has begun to throb with emotions of love. You, like a very powerful magnet, forcefully attract me towards you. You are the only girl who has excited my manly vigour. You must remember that life is a flower of which love is the honey. Love is not at all a bad thing. The world exists on love. If there is no love, the world will cease to exist. Many young and attractive girls had come in close contact with me in the past but none of them was able to arouse love in me.

Now I treat you as my sweetheart, my young and attractive beloved. I have completely lost myself to you. You are the winner and owner of my heart and soul. I have become your eternal slave. I love you most profoundly from the bottom of my heart. I shall never do anything against your wish. Everything will be done to please you. I shall fully obey you without hesitation. I shall never do anything without your prior permission. I want to have your pleasant company every moment. I most strongly desire to love you, and to be loved by you for ever. I am most ardently waiting for the day when I shall have you by my side. If you consent to my humble and most fervent appeal, I shall be most grateful and delighted. I shall be beside myself with joy.

Your parents will need a big amount of money if you want to marry somebody else. But if you agree to be my beloved, your parents will be saved from dowry and many other financial troubles. Am I right, Pushpa?

As my Mistress, you will have the scope to assist me in my business affairs. I am highly impressed by your intellectual ability, academic brilliance, efficient and smooth performance of duties, organising capacity and business acumen. Here it is worth mentioning that your sound and solid suggestions in the recent past had been found very valuable.

Now it is absolutely clear that you will be able to live a very happy and luxurious life as my beloved, and not as my Private Secretary.

I shall be extremely obliged if you very kindly reciprocate my love at the earliest.

With deepest love,

Yours ever,

Prem Kumar

(Full name and address of the recipient)

2. Negative reply

(Full address of the writer, and date)

Mr. Prem Kumar,

This morning I received your letter dated the 13th August 19....

I was terribly shocked and stunned to receive such a dirty letter from a man of your standing and status in the modern society of the twentieth century How did you stoop so low?

I was so far under the impression that I had been working in a renowned industrial organisation headed by a respectable and well educated gentleman. Now your letter presents you in your true colours. It fully reveals your fiendish (extremely bad or unpleasant) mentality and brutish desire.

It is completely clear from the letter that you are wholly bent upon buying my youth, love and beauty with your money and influence. Never dream of it. Forget it for ever.

You have thrown tremendous temptation to me in a shameless manner. Just remember that I am half your age. You should have treated me as your daughter. You should feel extremely ashamed of what you have penned in the nasty letter. You have thrown all decency to the winds.

What do you think of the poor? Do you think that the poor have no self-respect? How dare you cast aspersion on my character? What you have written, constitute a legal offence of a serious nature. You have thus lowered my reputation, status and standing in the estimation of the people. Besides, I have suffered horrible mental anguish. So I must not let you go scot-free. I have firmly and finally decided to teach you a very bitter lesson. I shall take legal action against you as early as possible.

I shall not attend your office with effect from tomorrow, the 14th August, 19... The amount due to me must be sent to me at the address given on the top right corner of this letter on or before the 7th of the next month without fail. Treat it as a letter of my formal resignation from the post of Private Secretary.

It is in the fitness of things to state that I am totally scared of your lewd intention. You amply deserve to be called a *Shaitan* of the worst type in the guise of a human being.

Yours faithfully,

Pushpa

(Full name and address of the recipient)

3. Affirmative reply

(Full address of the writer, and date)

Dear Prem Kumar,

I have just received your letter of the 13th instant. I thank you most profoundly for it.

Your letter was quite a surprise, a very agreeable one. You have paid me the greatest compliment any girl can receive. The least I can do is to try to give you my answer promptly and frankly. It is, however, a very difficult matter to collect my thoughts at a time like this. I hardly know how to put those thoughts on paper.

I must tell you candidly that, for a long time now, I have liked you and indeed thought very highly of you. When it became apparent that you were excessively interested in me, I prayed I might prove worthy of you. I am glad that we have known each other for so long a period. Honestly speaking, the contents of your letter have gladdened me beyond expression in language. I do not find adequate words to express the depth of my delight. In a word, I am beside myself with joy. I find it extremely hard to describe my feelings since the arrival of your letter.

I can tell you now that I have loved you very dearly ever since I had started working for you. Now, however, I feel I can safely and honestly say *Yes* to the question your letter asks. I think I must be the happiest girl alive. I am very proud that you have asked me to be your Mistress. Let me assure you from the core of my heart that my whole life will be passed in trying to show you how real and true my love is.

I cannot find words to express what is in my heart. You must come immediately on receipt of this letter. I shall count the minutes until you arrive. I have told father that you are coming to see me. He will, I am sure, be glad to see you. Of course, you will explain something of your plans for the future. I know he will help us as far as he is able.

I hope this finds you all at home in the best of health and happiness.

Yours ever,

Pushpa

(Full name and address of the recipient)

4. Letter of apology from a lover to his beloved

(Full address of the writer, and date)

Dearest Premlata,

First let me candidly and completely admit that I was responsible for the row I had with you over a trifle last evening when we were having a stroll in the park. Now I fully realise that I was really off my head and I totally lost my temper. I feel extremely ashamed of the fact that I used a few indecent words in the course of our heated argument. I did so in a fit of anger. I have fully realised my utter folly. I should not have done so.

Darling, believe me what I say. I could not have even a wink of sleep last night. I kept tossing on the bed. I am extremely sorry for my foolishness. I could not have my dinner last night. I should not have created the ugly and shameful scene. I most bitterly repent my unbecoming behaviour. Words fail me to express the depth of my mental agony. In a word, I am feeling like a fish out of water.

I vividly remember that you have always been very kind, nice, fine, considerate and sympathetic to me. I am most grateful to you for what you have been doing for my pleasure in every possible way for so long a period. I love you most intensely. My profound love for you really beggars description. I can never afford to lose your love. I shall never be able to live without you even for a moment. I swear by God, the Greatest, that I shall never do anything to annoy you. I sincerely offer you my deepest apology. I entreat (earnestly request) you to forgive me and to forget the past.

I shall continue to love you most dearly till the last moment of my life. I do hope you will very kindly give me one more chance. Please meet me tomorrow at 4-30 p.m. at the very place where we have been meeting for over six months. I am sure you will never disappoint me.

With most profound love,

Yours for ever,

Nitish

(Full name and address of the recipient)

5. Reply to the above

(Full address of the writer, and date)

My dear Nitish,

I have just now received your letter of the 6th May, ... I am deeply delighted to know that you love me so passionately that you cannot live without me even for a moment. Know it for certain that I do not lag behind. I also love you most profoundly. I assure you I am yours. Nothing can separate me from you in any circumstances.

Nitish, I totally forgot the ugly, unexpected and unpleasant incident even while I was on my way home. I never took it seriously. We must remember that such trifling happenings do take place in the course of love affairs. We must ignore them. The path of love is always strewn with thorns, and we must tread cautiously. Nothing should be allowed to interfere with our pure, true and profound love for each other. This is why I want you to never take such things to heart. Let bygones be bygones.

Nitish darling, I have fully forgiven you. Please take it for granted that I shall, as usual, meet you at that very place daily at 4-30 p.m. You have nothing to worry about. Be in good cheer.

With all my love,

Your loving and devoted,

Premlata

(Full name and address of the recipient)

6. Beloved breaks off engagement with her lover

(Full address of the writer, and date)

My dear Piyus,

I hasten to tell you that I quiver as I write it. The urgency of the matter compels me to pen and send it to you just now. This is a matter of far-reaching importance concerning both of us. Honestly speaking, I do not know how to go about it in a proper manner. I know you will be shocked and stunned to read the contents of the letter.

I have firmly and finally decided to break off my engagement with you with immediate effect. This is my irrevocable decision. It can never be reversed. This painful decision of mine will surely be good for both of us. Let me spell out the cogent reasons for this heart-breaking and heart-rending action. Of late, I have observed that both of us have totally different interests and temperaments. This is nothing but a simple and pure truth that the warmth of love which we had for each other at the beginning has gradually dried out. Besides, we had been quite indifferent and cold to each other on many an occasion in the recent past. This is why I have made up my mind not to love you any longer. I do not want to be an unwilling partner of your love. Now it is absolutely clear that it will never be easy for us to live a happy and peaceful life if we get married.

I am returning all your presents and letters along with this letter. When you find time, please return the letters which, I had written to you.

I am sorry to disappoint you.

Yours sincerely,

Purnima

(Full name and address of the recipient)

7. Reply to the above

(Full address of the writer, and date)

My dear Purnima,

I have got your letter informing me of your firm and final decision to break off your engagement with me. This has totally broken my heart. I am completely confused. My mental anguish babbles expression in language. Purnima, I never did anything to you to deserve such a severe punishment. Please do not get angry with me when I say that what you have mentioned as the causes compelling you to end our relationship are not at all true. I can say with confidence that you have acted against me on the basis of mere misunderstanding.

Parvati, my former beloved, must have poisoned your ears against me. I had been in deep love with her till about four months ago. At present, she is a very bitter enemy of mine. She is an extremely cunning, mean, selfish, greedy, undesirable and unreliable person. She is jealous of my love-affair with you. She does not want me to love you. She had betrayed and cheated her former lovers with no exception. She very much loves young men who are healthy and wealthy. But her preference is for one who is tall, and strong and stout.

My love-affair with her did not last even nine months. During the period I had been her passionate lover, I had given her more than ten thousand rupees and many dear (expensive) gifts, but she had never given me anything in return.

I had all along hoped that you and I would be united in wedlock and we would lead a happy and peaceful married life. Now you have completely shattered all my hopes. I never imagined that this could be the end of our true and pure love-affair, and that you would ruin my life in such a merciless manner. Truly speaking, I find it extremely hard to believe what you have penned in the letter.

I never thought that we were drifting away from each other. I also never sensed even the slightest inkling of what you had in your mind with regard to my intense love for you. Darling, despite all this, I still love you very dearly. I shall always remain absolutely faithful and sincere to you.

I shall never be able to live without you even for a day. Life without you will be wholly hopeless and worthless for me. I am fully prepared to sacrifice everything for the sake of your love for me.

I most earnestly request you to take pity on me, and not to leave me. If you do not change your decision, I shall never marry anybody else till the last moment of my life. In that event, I shall have to live the life of a celibate (unmarried person).

I am keenly awaiting your early and favourable reply.

With sweet memories of the past,

Yours for ever,

Piyus

(Full name and address of the recipient)

8. Beloved's reply

(Full address of the writer, and date)

Dear Piyus,

I was out of station for two weeks. That was why I could not send a prompt reply to your letter of the 2nd May, 19.... I hope you will not mind this inordinate delay on my part.

I hasten to thank you profoundly for your warm feelings which you have expressed in your letter. I deem it expedient to assure you that I had taken the decision after a great deal of heart-searching. All the relevant pros and cons were minutely taken into consideration. It is most regretted that the decision already taken is irrevocable. I am wholly helpless in the matter. Please treat it as final.

Let me reiterate that I shall never marry you. Now the best thing for you to do is to forget me as well as the past for ever. I am extremely sorry that this action of mine has deeply disappointed and pained you.

Yours Sincerely,

Purnima

(Full name and address of the recipient)

9. *Love letter from a bachelor to a young widow*

(Full address of the writer, and date)

My dear Padmini,

Perhaps you will be surprised to receive this letter.

It may be recalled that we had occasions to meet each other in the past. It was on the last occasion that I could read the anxiety writ large on your beautiful face. I fully understand your horrible worries. You are so young, so beautiful, so intelligent, so sweet and yet without any proper protection.

It is really unfortunate, nay tragic, that a young woman like you should become a widow at such a young and tender age.

You know that I am still a bachelor without much family obligation. I had decided to lead a bachelor's life in pursuit of knowledge and learning, but your innocent, full-moon-like face clouded with worries and insecurity has urged me to change my decision. I have thoroughly pondered over the matter, and finally, I have decided to marry you. It is not at all out of pity that I am penning(writing) this letter. This is also not meant to injure your sentiments in any way. Actually I highly admire your grace and grand manners. To speak the truth, I am in deep love with you.

It is needless to say that love is the best remedy for all troubles. In recent months, I too have been feeling lonely and emotionally insecure. It is really tragic to be left alone in this materialistic world which is full of woes and misery. No disease is so disastrous as the sense of being unloved and unwanted. It is also worth noting with great delight that our union in wedlock will have tremendous aesthetic potential. Because you are a good artist and I am a noted author. We shall positively make an ideal couple by all means. I shall be glad to love you dearly, to serve you, to provide you with social status, name and security. Your little daughter will be treated as my own daughter. I shall be proud to shower my affection on her. Under our care and guidance, she will ultimately grow into a beautiful lady, and will have a bright career.

There is no hurry. You can take your own time. You can come to a conclusion after taking all the relevant facts into due consideration. If my proposal stirs your inner self, and if you really feel an attachment for me, kindly reply. If not, please forget it for ever.

Think twice before you decide, but remember that you need someone who may really love you, protect you against the odds of life. On my part, I do confess that I love you deeply and I need you. Let me have a chance to prove my worth.

With profound love,

Yours,

Sanjay

(Full name and address of the recipient)

10. Lover refuses to forget his beloved.

(Full address of the writer, and date)

My dear Laxmi,

I totally fail to understand as to why you asked me to forget you for ever. I never did anything to you to call for such a drastic action against me. Why should I forget you ? Know it for certain that it is absolutely impossible for me to forget you even for a moment. I can forget everything under the sun but I can never forget you. I must frankly tell you that nothing in the world can force or persuade me to forget you.

You are my life and soul. Life without you is totally unimaginable. Don't you know that I love you most dearly ? My love for you is selfish. I cannot breathe without you. Please take it for granted that if you leave me, I am sure to die of heart failure. It will surely be a sin on your part to cause my death for which God, the Greatest, will never forgive you.

For God's sake, never ask me again to forget you. Don't you remember that you had, in the past, promised many times that you would marry me and be mine for good ? You must abide by your solemn promise made in the name of God. You must not go back on your promise. Promises are always meant to be acted upon, and not to be broken up at one's whims. Laxmi darling, kindly stick to your solemn promise.

I can never forget those golden days when we never separated from each other even for a second. Now I want you to kindly take the trouble to remember those sweet memories of the not-so-distant past.

I always dream of your beautiful face; big, blue and sparkling eyes; rosy cheeks; pink lips; long and pointed nose; slender waist and fingers; melodious voice; splendid gait; stunning beauty; polite and polished manners; balanced views; varied interests in academic field; sharp intellect; graceful gesture and marvellous elocution. Everything about you is pleasing, winsome and fairy-like. I assure you that I shall never be able to get rid of your image. Your are the light by which I live.

Laxmi dear, I swear that I shall continue to love you most passionately till the last moment of my life. I shall never do anything against your wish. Nothing will be done without your prior permission. Everything will be done to make you happy and cheerful. I throw myself before you like flowers in a temple to be lifted or trampled over. Now it is you who can save my life. Kindly confirm that you will continue to love me as before.

I am most keenly awaiting your reply at the earliest.

With all my love,

Yours,

Sewa Dass

(Full name and address of the recipient)

11. Reply to the above

(Full address of the writer, and date)

Dear Sewa Dass,

I have just got your letter of the 31st ultimo. I thank you for the expression of your cordial feelings for me.

I do not want to keep you in the dark even for a moment. Now everything has suddenly and completely changed. The circumstances are totally beyond my control. I cannot love you any longer. My firm decision is that I shall never marry you. I am entirely helpless in the matter.

The reason for all this is that after the sad and sudden demise of my dear and revered father, my eldest brother, Ganesh, has taken complete charge of the family. He is deadly against my love-affair with you. This is why you are earnestly requested to realise my utter helplessness in the matter, and to forget me for ever.

Yours sincerely,

Laxmi

(Full name and address of the recipient)

12. *Letter from a beloved scolding her lover for his silence*

(Full address of the writer, and date)

Dearest Vishnu,

How are you ? How are you getting along with your studies ? Your prolonged silence has actually bewildered me. I have not received any letter from you for about two months. You also did not bother to come and see me. It is mysterious. Why do you not write to me ? Have I done anything wrong ? I cannot help thinking that something must be wrong, because you are usually so prompt in visiting, and writing to me. I am worried beyond expression in language. Let me tell you that a man even with an atom of pretence to honour and good-breeding would not intentionally put a girl into the position you have placed me. You are constantly before my mind's eye. This inordinate silence on your part shocks me to madness. I totally fail to understand as to how an ardent and so vocal a lover like you has become dumb all at once.

I am being wasted day and night. Life has become a big burden. What should I do ? Will you honestly tell me what your silence means ? Have you fallen in love with some other beautiful girl of your choice? My strong suspicion is that another attractive damsel is delighting your tender heart. I want you to speak the truth. Never try to betray or befool me. You had sworn many a time to remain constant and faithful to me. Do you remember it? Let me know why you have turned so cruel.

I cannot think what it can be, as your last letter was so jolly and cheerful. I have read it repeatedly in order to make up for your other letters which have not been received by me. Do not keep me in suspense.

I cannot keep on begging you to reply to my letters. To be waiting day after day for letters which do not come, is much more than what I can bear. So this will be the last time you will hear from me, unless I receive your reply within four days. I shall forgive your extraordinary silence if you only write and explain everything in detail. If you fail to do so, I am sure to whither away like a flower.

You are the divine physician of my heart. Come and heal this love-sick beloved of yours. It is already well known to you that I have none else in this vast world to turn to, for help or guidance in this dark hour. There is none but you to understand my agony and suffering.

I cannot write more, because I am terribly miserable.

Your loving,

Mohini

(Full name and address of the recipient)

13. Letter from a fiancee to her fiance on the eve of his departure for Saudi Arabia

(Full address of the writer, and date)

My dearest Arjun,

I hope you will get this letter before the plane leaves the Calcutta airport. Perhaps it will comfort you to know that there is someone here praying fervidly for your safety on the outward flight, and during your stay in Saudi Arabia.

I wish I could come down and see you off, and once again tell you how I shall miss you. But something beyond my control prevents me from doing so. This is why I must content myself by writing.

Arjun, I shall miss you very miserably. I shall count the months and the days until you come back. It is only a matter of hours since we said good-bye, but it seems to me as if many days have already gone by. Honestly speaking, I feel as though I shall hardly be able to stand your separation from me, but, for your sake, I am going to try to be brave.

I shall hope and pray that sound health and splendid success attend you during your stay abroad. I want you to promise that you will pen to me at least twice a month, and that you will fully describe your experiences at the various places you visit. Do you know what your letters mean to me ? They will be my only joy in a very weary time of waiting. They will charm away the weariness of waiting.

May God bless you and keep you safe and sound.

Good-bye, Arjun darling.

Your loving and devoted,

Parvati

(Full name and address of the recipient)

14. Letter of protest from a girl to her sweetheart

(Full address of the writer, and date)

My dearest Ram Mehar,

I hardly know how to begin this letter. I have lately observed that your interest in me has been rapidly lessening. Now your interest in me has almost no real existence. Can you deny the fact that nowadays you visit me very seldom and never spend the evening in my company as you used to do? When I express a wish of any kind, it seems to fall on a deaf ear. How has such a change come about? Can you give me a satisfactory explanation?

I have never been fastidious or jealous or exacting. I never bothered you when I saw that you were tired, or wished to visit your other friends instead of coming to me. I fear that there is something wrong which will make my tender heart ache.

Do you remember that when you first came to see me it was with a smile and a willing step? You were impatient until we met each other, and when we met, you thought that the time flew all too quickly. Now your step is slow, and there is no smile; and the time hangs heavy.

The unexpected change on your part has been noticed not only by me but also by all the members of our family. Everybody has expressed much surprise at it. But how can I explain when I myself am in the dark? Is it that you are tired of coming to me, and wish to break off the engagement, or are you in trouble of any kind? If you wish to leave me, you have only to speak and you are free. If it be trouble, why not tell me and let me try and help you? You are sadly mistaken if you think that I would care for you less, were you poorer. Do not think me a bar to another attachment.

Write and tell me what I am to think. This dreadful suspense is more than what I can bear.

Still your own,

Renu

(Full name and address of the recipient)

15. Lover is anxious for an early meeting with his sweetheart

(Full address of the writer, and date)

Dearest Anandi,

How are you ? How are you getting along with your studies ? You have not met me for ten days. You also have not replied to my letter of the 10th instant. Consequently, I am very anxious about your health. What is the matter with you ? I fail to understand whether you are annoyed with, or indifferent to, me. I have not done anything to annoy you even in the least. I entreat you not to be so cruel to me. I remember you every second. I am feeling like a fish out of water.

I am extremely eager to meet you. Anandi, I earnestly request you to meet me on Sunday next at that very place at 4-30 p.m. positively. I shall surely and gladly await you till you come. I do hope you will not disappoint me.

With boundless love,

Yours for ever,

Umesh

(Full name and address of the recipient)

16. Reply to the above

(Full address of the writer, and date)

My dear Umesh,

Thank you for your letter of the 18th instant which I got this morning.

You have no need to cry like a child or to be disappointed. I have repeatedly told you not to worry about me if I fail to meet you even for twenty days at a stretch. Some trusted and tested admirers had come from different, distant places to see me without prior appointment. Naturally I had to spend my time with, and entertain, them as long as they stayed with me. That was why I could not write to, or meet, you despite my best longing. Really speaking, I am very sorry for the anxiety caused to you. I request you not to mind the inordinate delay on my part in this regard.

Umesh, do not forget that I also have a tender heart. I love you very dearly. Know it for certain that I shall never lag behind in this respect.

I am sure you will be jumping with joy to know that I shall positively meet you on Sunday next as so keenly and kindly desired by you.

With all my love,

Yours,

Anandi

(Full name and address of the writer)

17. Beloved requests lover to meet her parents

(Full address of the writer, and date)

My dear Shiv,

How are you? How are you getting along with your multifarious activities?

We have been in deep love with each other for over a couple of years. We have closely known each other's nature, interests and views. We are postgraduates, intelligent, wise and mature enough to live a happy and peaceful life. In my opinion, it is now time for us to be united in wedlock. We should not wait any longer. I love you so intensely that I want to be with you all the time. I am absolutely unable to live separately from you any longer.

It is the most opportune moment for you to talk over this matter with my parents. They like you, and you have nothing to be afraid of. They will certainly give you a reply in the affirmative. Do not waste even a minute. Do not hesitate at all. Summon up courage, hurry up and call on them at the earliest, and make a formal proposal for my marriage with you.

This is my sound and sincere advice. Please act upon it at once. Do not brood over the matter. The need of the hour is that you take up this delicate matter with them in right earnest with no loss of time. Otherwise all our long-cherished hopes will be shattered once for all.

Let us have unflinching faith in God, and proceed in our lifelong mission with firm determination. Our sincere efforts will surely be crowned with success, because our love is true and pure. Besides, we are made for each other.

With all my love and solemn prayers,

Your most loving and devoted,

Shakuntala

(Full name and address of the recipient)

18. Reply to the above

(Full address of the writer, and date)

My dear Shakuntala,

I am deeply delighted to receive your sweet letter of the 8th instant. I fully agree with you on your sound, sincere and timely advice. I am also absolutely unable to bear this separation from you any longer.

I shall definitely call on your dear and revered parents within four days and tell them everything in detail. I shall entreat them to allow you to marry me. I am sanguine about success in my sacred mission.

With all my love and best wishes,

Yours for ever,

Shiv

(Full name and address of the recipient)

19. Letter from wife to her husband away from home

(Full address of the writer, and date)

Dearest Bharat,

I am beside myself with joy to receive your sweet letter. I had a sudden and severe attack of malarial fever. That was why I could not reply to it in time. I am sorry for the delay. Now I have fully got well. You need not worry about me at all. Your letter has completely charmed away all my troubles and worries.

The fact that you remember me so much, has gladdened me beyond expression in language. I always yearn for your constant company. I cannot think of anything else. Words fail me to express the depth of my delight. I have already read your letter five times and still I feel like reading it time and again. I had been feeling depressed for the last few days but your letter has helped me in getting rid of that mood. The letter has again reminded me how lucky I am to have such a loving and understanding husband.

You left home only twenty-five days ago but it seems to me as if a span (period) of twenty-five months has rolled by (passed). I thrilled at the good news that you would be back home by the middle of this month. I am getting impatient. Do not defer your departure for here. I love you most deeply.

I have bought an exquisite present for you. I shall tell you nothing about it here. It will be ceremoniously presented to you on your return home. I know you will like and admire it very much.

Bharat darling, I want you to take the trouble to write to me once a week. A line from you will surely keep me in high spirits. In case, you fail to do so, I shall not be able to bear your separation from me.

I miss you very miserably. If possible, try to come home once a month during holidays. How are you getting along with your office work? I shall keep on counting the days till you come back home.

I hope this finds you quite hale and hearty.

With lots of love and millions of kisses.

Yours,

Savitri

(Fulll name and address of the recipient)

20. Reply to the above

(Full address of the writer, and date)

Dearest Savitri,

I am glad beyond words to receive your charming letter of the 22nd instant.

I am overjoyed at the news that you have wholly recovered from your illness. Please take care of your health.

I always cherish your sweet memory in my mind. You are the dearest and loveliest of all things to me. I love you so much that I think of you every moment. Your sweet letters are the only source of joy in my loneliness at this distant place.

The end of the current financial year is drawing near. So I am very busy with my office work. Despite all this, I promise that I shall write to you once a week as fondly desired by you. I shall always do my best to make you happy and cheerful at any cost.

I have fully realised that life without you is boring, dull

and drab. I very badly feel the pangs of your separation from me. You willl be deeply delighted to know that I am coming home to celebrate a happy and bright Diwali with you. Thus we shall have the golden opportunity to enjoy a pleasant time together for a few days.

I shall also surprise you with a pleasing and precious present.

With deepest love,

Yours for ever,

Bharat

(Full name and address of the recipient)

21. Letter from a girl's father warning a young man

To,

(Full address of the writer, and date)

Mr .....

(Full address)

Sir,

My eldest daughter, Rani, has shown me your letter of the 22nd of the last month.

You have written, among other things, that you love her most intensely. She tells me that she has, on several occasions, asked you not to write to her again. She has also informed me that you take every possible opportunity to force your presence upon her.

I, therefore, feel it my duty to request you neither to write to her again nor to embarrass her in any way. You would do well to make a due note of the fact that it is quite impossible for her to look upon you in any other light than as a mere acquaintance.

I trust you will fully realise the gravity of the matter. It is in your own interest to accept this letter as final and comply with my request. I am sure you will not compel me to take steps that will be highly distasteful to me and excessively detrimental to your future.

Yours faithfully,

Ram Chand

22. Letter from a lover to his beloved proposing marriage

(Full address of the writer, and date)

My dearest Chanchala,

How are you ? How are you getting alongwith your office work? I do not know how many times I have complained in my letters about our continued separation. I think that you have guessed by now that there is a pretty deep reason behind this complaint. This separation is more irksome at the moment than it has ever been. The reason for this is that I do not feel able to put off any longer asking you a question that I had been hoping to put in different circumstances. I think you know what is coming, so here it is: darling, will you marry me ?

You know that I love you very dearly, and that since we met five months ago, my feelings have got even stronger. I could not ask you then, because we had not known each other long.

Secondly, I expected to be home again soon. I meant to wait until I got back but I just cannot.

I know that I cannot offer you much. Goodness knows how much longer I shall be stuck out here. But there must be an end of it soon. The waiting will be less dreary if I can think that the end will be the beginning of a new life with you as my wife.

Know it for certain that I love you from the core of my heart, and I want you very much.

Yours for ever,

Nakul

(Full name and address of the recipient)

23. *Affirmative reply*

(Full address of the writer, and date)

My dearest Nakul,

Oh, yes, yes, YES.

But that is just to confirm my telegram with the same words, which you should get today.

Was it improper on my part to send a wire accepting your proposal of marriage with so much gusto? You gave me a pretty broad hint in your previous letter, and when I replied, I tried to give you the green light. Now I shall make you proud and tell you that I tried to talk to you on the phone five minutes after I got your last letter, but in vain.

Nakul, I know you cannot name the day. I am as fed up about this separation as you are. It is no good asking you to be patient because I am terribly impatient myself. We must just hope and dream.

Father and mother are writing to you separately. They need a little time for this sort of thing, but I can tell you that now they are very pleased. I cannot tell you how I feel . At the moment, I am just in a flap (in a state of confusion) with tremendous excitement, and I cannot even eat. Nakul darling, I love you so much.

I shall write again when I have calmed down a bit.

Yours,

Chanchala

(Full name and address of the recipient)

24. Negative reply

(Full address of the writer, and date)

My dearest Nakul,

You have paid me the greatest compliment any girl can receive. The least I can do, is to give you my answer promptly and frankly.

Nakul, I am afraid the answer is *no*.

After reading your letter, I felt guilty. It never occurred to me that you were leading up to this in your previous letters, and if I seemed to give you encouragement I assure you that it was not intended. If we had been seeing each other instead of just writing, I am sure this would never have happened.

I owe you a reason at least for this refusal. It would be easy for me to say that we did not know each other long enough, or that I am not really sure about my feelings towards you. But that would be unfair. It might make you go on wasting your hopes on me; and they would be wasted.

Nakul, please do not take it too much to heart when I tell you bluntly that I shall never be your wife. I like you tremendously — more than any other man I know. But I am not in love with you.

Nakul, I like and admire you. I have risked hurting your feelings because I do not want you to waste your time hoping that I shall change. I know I shall not change. And I know you will find someone much better fitted to be your wife than I am.

I hope you will always think of me as,

Your very sincere friend,

Chanchala

(Full name and address of the recipient)

25. Letter from a beloved postponing an answer to a proposal of marriage

(Full address of the writer, and date)

My dearest Ramesh,

I have just received your letter asking me to marry you, and now I am expected to write back *yes* or *no*. Ramesh, I cannot. I like you tremendously —— you know that; but I honestly do not know whether I love you. I did not know you long enough while you were still in Kuwait. I shall not really know how I feel until I see you again.

The other side of the picture is that you may find that I am not quite all you imagine because you cannot see me, and I should hate you to come back and find that you did not love your fiancee after all.

If I seemed to encourage you to make a proposal, I am very sorry.

I know that this *she did not say yes, did not say no* business is unsatisfactory. I know that a time may come when I shall regret it. But I cannot see any alternative.

May I make a suggestion? Let us go on writing to each other as before, and see how it works out. If either of us meets anyone else, the other has no claim.

A last word, Ramesh. I have not met anyone else yet. If I do, I shall tell you at once. I expect you to do the same. Because this is my risk as well as yours.

Yours ever,

Ranjana

(Full name and address of the recipient)

26. Letter from a fiance to his fiancee who has been angry with him

(Full address of the writer, and date)

My dearest Santoshi,

We have always agreed to be absolutely frank and truthful to each other. I am not going to pretend to be a penitent sinner now, because I do not feel one. You were cross (angry) with me, and as I told you, I thought you were unfair. I still think so, though I realise that I did not help matters by the way I took it.

I do not mind admitting that I have felt much fed up with life since our row. I wanted to make it up, but I know you would not think much of me if I tried to win you back by pretending to take all the blame. I am of the opinion that it is about fifty-fifty, and I hope you will agree to forget the whole thing that existed.

Darling, I love you as much as I ever did. When can I come round and kiss and make up?

Your loving,

Arvind

(Full name and address of the recipient)

27. Reply to the above

(Full address of the writer, and date)

My dearest Arvind,

You have made me feel an absolutely ill-mannered person. I have been trying to pen to you ever since our row, and it was only silly false pride that prevented me from doing so.

I do not agree that the blame was fifty-fifty, or anything like that. It was my fault, but if it is any consolation to you, I have felt utterly miserable ever since.

I think you are a darling, and I do not deserve you. Please come as fast as you can for the make-up kiss.

Your loving,

Santoshi

(Full name and address of the recipient)

28. Letter from a lover breaking off an engagement

(Full address of the writer, and date)

Dear Manju,

It is with great reluctance that I am about to perform what I feel to be a duty to you and to myself.

I have to tell you that I realise that I no longer love you. Indeed, I am not certain that I ever loved in the way you so well deserve to be loved.

What can I say in explanation? Only this: you are such a charming person that, quite unconsciously, you draw others to yourself almost against their will. Any man, who is thrown constantly in your society, as I have been, might, after a time, imagine that he loved you.

But circumstances have recently revealed to me the true feeling I have for you, and I am very sure that it is not love.

I do not think I should have had the courage to tell you this, were it not that I have never been whole heartedly certain of your love for me.

You see, it is second nature with you to be gracious and kind to all men, and this fact may have deceived me.

I firmly believe it is so, and that is releasing me from the engagement there will be no lasting sorrow on your part; only, as with me, a passing regret.

While wishing you abundant happiness in the future, may I ask you always to think of me as

Your sincere friend,

Anath

(Full name and address of the recipient)

29. Letter from a man offering his fiancee her freedom

(Full address of the writer, and date)

My dearest Kamlesh,

This is a difficult letter to write. The facts are that, of late, I have been wondering if you care for me as you used to do. I may be entirely wrong, and I sincerely hope I am, but on a number of occasions I have noticed little incidents which seemed to show that my presence displeased you.

I can honestly say that my affection for you has not changed or grown less in any way and that I want you as much as I ever did. But this is the point. It is utter folly to go on if you are growing cold. I want you to be happy and I want you to be happy with me, but unless you can assure me that you are not changing, it would certainly be better to call our engagement off.

So, Kamlesh, do be perfectly honest and tell me if I am right or wrong.

Yours ever,
Sachin

(Full name and address of the recipient)

30. Letter from a girl asking a young man to refrain from pursuing his unwanted attentions

(Full address of the writer, and date)

To

Mr....

(Full address)

Dear Sir,

I find it necessary to write to you on a matter which has caused me some worry recently. I refer to your persistent and, to me, distasteful attentions.

I do not think I have ever given you any encouragement, and I am hoping that, on reading this expression of my feelings, your good taste will prompt you to desist from what I wholly and rightly consider an embarrassing annoyance.

Yours truely

Urmila Devi

31. Letter from a beloved to her lover explaining a misunderstanding

(Full address of the writer, and date)

Dearest Dinesh,

It is my firm belief that you surely never thought that I was guilty of *flirting* with a stranger .possessing a strong and stout physique at the Ashoka Hotel, even though a report was spread to that effect. Yet the tone of your letter, more than your words, seems to imply that you accepted the statement as true, without even asking me, whom you say you trust, for an explanation. My dear, it hurts me to think that you are capable of doubting me, because I fear there is unhappiness in store for us both of you listen to and believe every little bit of tittle-tattle or gossip.

I shall tell you exactly what happened. Mr. Anil has recently returned from Riyadh, the capital of Saudi Arabia, where he saw Sunil, my elder brother, who gave him a letter of introduction to my father. I saw Mr. Anil on the night of his arrival at the Ashoka Hotel. I was introduced to him as Sunil's sister. Was it not natural that I should inquire for my brother and ask him a few questions about him (Sunil)? I was interested, not in the man himself but in the news of my brother, and listened eagerly as he told it. The ill-natured report that reached your ears, probably arose from my attention to it.

I have given you this explanation because I feel you were not really yourself when you wrote. Write to me at once, my Dinesh darling, and say that you never believed what was said to you.

Your own,

Sunita

(Full name and address of the recipient.)

32. Letter from a girl chiding her fiance for flirting at a party

(Full address of the writer, and date)

My dearest Ashoke,

I think I shall be wanting (deficient) in self-respect if I do not write you a few lines of remonstrance (protest) respecting (concerning) your open flirtation with Miss Sundari last night.

Everybody noticed it, many mentioned it, and it was very unpleasant for me to hear remarks about your behaviour towards her.

Were you not *engaged* to me, I should, of course, have had no right to object. But in view of our long-standing friendship, it would have deeply hurt me. But under the circumstances in which we are placed, I was extremely annoyed.

If your engagement to me is irksome let it, by all means, be ended, but do end it in an open and honest way. Do not, dearest Ashoke, attempt to undermine my affection by such public displays of indifference. It was open to me, I know, to have danced and amused myself also, as you indeed hinted at the time. But you forgot that a girl cannot make public displays of either indifference or affection. I was obliged, for your sake, as well as my own, to hide my real feelings. I was determined not to give you any excuse for what I considered your cruel and outrageous conduct to me.

While we are engaged, I think that right feeling and common courtesy, at any rate, demand that I should be treated with more consideration.

I hope to hear that you are penitent.

Yours,
Radha Rani

(Full name and address of the recipient)

33. Letter from a lover to his sweetheart.

(Full address of the writer, and date)

My dearest Uma,

I have just received your delightful letter of the 4th of this month. It is very sweet of you to pen to me so often. You have my most profound thanks. While we are separated, as we must be for a few months, your letters bring me something of your dear self. Although I treasure them very highly, they are a poor recompense for your absence. Still I am most thankful for small mercies, as people say. I very eagerly look forward to your letters with more impatience than you can magine. So you must make it convenient to drop me a few lines as often as you can.

I often wonder if other people whom we see around us love as we love each other. Do they know the joys of meeting and the sorrows of parting as we do ?

Let me tell you the simple and pure truth. As I look at them, I pity each one. The reason is not far to seek. I, with smug satisfaction in my heart, know that few are loved as I am. Do others understand love as we know it? Do all lovers talk as we do? It they do, the world must be a very happy place.

There is hardly an hour I do not think of you in some way or other. If I see flowers, I want to give them to you. If I see beauty, I want you to admire it too. If I meet a fine thought in a book, I want you to share it. If I am worried, I want your help and sympathy. My darling, You have made yourself a necessity to my life. I shall never be content until we are united in wedlock.

With all my love,

Your very loving and devoted,

Rishi Raj

(Full name and address of the recipient)

34. Letter from a maid servant accusing her lover with neglect

(Full address of the writer, and date)

My dear Paresh,

I have not heard from you for nearly two months, although I posted four letters to you. I thought that you had gone out of station with your employer. Suresh called at our house day before yesterday. He told me that you were still in town. I think it is very unkind of you to leave my letters so long unanswered, more especially as you know how eagerly I wait for your letters. You must not suppose that I can sit down quietly and patiently under such treatment.

Do you remember the promises you have so often made to marry me ? You must bear it in mind that promises are made to be kept and not to be broken. You must abide by your promise. The suspense is becoming unbearable. Please let me know the cause of your silence as soon as possible.

Yours,

Nalini

(Full name and address of the recipient)

35. Letter from a maid servant replying a cool letter from her lover

(Full address of the writer, and date)

Dear Pranab,

I can hardly believe you wrote the letter which I received

this morning. It is so different from any of the others which I have from you. You must have either deceived me greatly, on your character has strangely altered for the worse during the last two months. Do you remember telling me over and over again that nothing would change your feelings towards me? And yet you write as coldly as though we were mere acquaintances. I shall not again ask you the reason of the change, because, if you have not, I have some little self-respect.

You wish, I think, to be free to marry another girl, and, instead of telling me in a manly way that such is the case, you coolly try to shake me off.

Your letter hardly deserved an answer, and I do not think I would have answered it, were it not my wish to tell you that you are no longer anything to me and need never write to me again.

Yours sincerely,

Usha

(Full name and address of the recipient)

36. Letter from a girl to her father announcing a proposal of marriage made to her

(Full address of the writer and date)

Dearest Father,

I have something very important to tell you. I hope you will be pleased when you have read my news. As you know, Manohar and I have been good friends for about two years. He has now made a proposal of marriage. Father, he is an awfully nice boy and I like and love him very much indeed. Manohar is in a good position, which he will explain when you meet him. You have told me that I should always follow the dictates of conscience, and my conscience is quite at ease about Manohar. I have, therefore, said to him that I shall be his wife, provided you give your assent.

He will come home with me on Friday and, I do hope you will give your consent to our engagement.

With fond love,

Your very affectionate daughter,

Nisha

(Full name and address of the recipient)

37. Affirmative answer from a maid servant to her lover's proposal of marriage

(Full address of the writer, and date)

My dearest Satish,

I hardly thought you cared for me sufficiently to ask me to become your wife. I admit you were very attentive when we were both at Nirmala's birthday party, but I never really imagined that you were in earnest. It appears that I have been doing you a great injustice, and the only way I can see to repair it is to say that I know no one whom I care for more than yourself.

We need, however, be in no hurry, as our savings put together are not very large yet. It would not be wise to leave good places until we have sufficient financial resources to begin some small business which would keep the wolf from the door. However, we can talk matters over more fully when we meet and I shall look forward to seeing you at the Ashoka Hotel on Sunday next at 5-30 p.m.

Yours affectionately,

Shashi

(Full name and address of the recipient)

38. Negative answer from a maid servant to her lover's proposal of marriage

(Full address of the writer, and date)

Dear Suresh,

You know as well as I do that I have never given you any encouragement, yet you ask me to marry you. Do you think I could marry a man whom I have always tried to avoid?

I am sure you have mistaken my character if you suppose that I am so anxious to be married as to accept a person whom I do not respect, for the sake of his money. Keep your money, Satish, and look out elsewhere, because my mind is firmly made up to remain single for a long time to come, and if I ever encourage a fellow-servant to speak to me, he must have better qualities than you possess.

Yours sincerely,

Raj Bala

(Full name and address of the recipient)

39. Letter from a man to his fiancee

(Full address of the writer, and date)

Dearest Kamini,

How are you ?

Do you remember that there are 45 days still left for our wedding ? It is a long period. Is it not ?

Kamini, time hangs very heavy upon me. I hope this is the same case with you too. I shudder to think that we have to wait for so long a period. It is definitely and exceedingly boring. The intensity of boredom can be lessened to a great extent. But everything wholly depends upon you. In my opinion, there will be no harm if both of us go for outing once a week. We are responsible persons. We are highly educated, wise and mature enough to protect our reputation. We shall never go beyond the bounds of decency.

Let us meet on every Sunday at 4-30 p.m. for a couple of hours only. I shall thus have the long cherished opportunity for spending some time in your sweet company. Secondly, we can discuss various topics of our mutual interest over a cup of hot coffee at one of the best restaurants in the city. You will surely be able to be back home much before sunset. I shall never request you to remain with me after 6-30 p.m.

Kamini, I always think of you every moment. Please know it for certain that my intense and pure love for you is much more than what I can express in writing.

Will you kindly take the trouble to convey my best respects to your dear and revered parents ?

I hope this finds you all at home quite hale and hearty.

I am eagerly awaiting your prompt reply.

With all my love,

Yours,

Santosh Kumar

(Full name and address of the recipient)

40. Reply to the above

(Full address of the writer, and date)

Dearest Santosh

I thank you most profoundly for your affectionate letter of the 4th instant sent to me through your youngest sister.

I assure you from the core of my heart that the contents of the letter have delighted me beyond expression in language. I highly value your pure and deep love for me. I also love you most dearly. I always think of you. I have shown your letter to mother. She has, in turn, shown it to father. After a thorough discussion over the matter, they have decided not to allow me to move out with you till our marriage ceremoney is solemnised. You will, I am sure, kindly realise that I am absolutely helpless in the matter. I am extremely sorry for it. I want you not to take it to heart.

Please make it convenient to write to me once a week.

I hope this finds you in the best of health and happiness.

With my deepest love,

Your loving and devoted,

Kamini

(Full name and address of the recipient)

41. Letter from a rejected suitor

(Full address of the writer, and date)

My dear Poonam,

It is useless for me to pretend that your letter was not a great blow to me, but at the same time I must confess that I had the feeling that your answer to my proposal of marriage would be in the negative. Truly speaking, at the moment I feel as though I shall not be able to bear the grief caused by your refusal to my proposal of marriage, because you are very dear to me. But I shall try to bear my profound grief like a man.

It will, I think, be better for both of us if we do not meet each other again for a few months. Thereafter we shall, I hope, be able to meet again as really good friends. Poonam, your happiness means so much to me that, if I know you are happy, I shall surely come to look upon the world as a place which is not quite so lonesome and cold as it seems at this moment.

I hope this finds you in the best of spirits.

Your sincere friend,

Pankaj

(Full name and address of the recipient)

42. Lover is puzzled by his beloved's whimsical behaviour

(Full address of the writer, and date)

My dear Nirdoshi,

Let me tell you frankly at the very outset that your

whimsical behaviour has puzzled me to a great extent.

You can never deny the fact that sometimes you become very friendly as if you are full of most passionate love for me, and at other times you become very cold and indifferent to me as if I have only a nodding acquaintance with you. It is extremely bad on your part to behave with me in such an improper manner. You must not forget that I am your great lover for a period of a little over two years. Please take me at my word when I say that I am absolutely unable to understand you.

Now I turn to myself. I love you most intensely. My love for you is pure and true. I shall never forget you. I shall never do anything against your wish. Everything will be done to please you. I shall always remain absolutely sincere and faithful to you.

Here it will be in the fitness of things to let you know something about my past experience gained in the field of love-affairs. Many beautiful attractive, ultra-modern and well educated girls belonging to rich families had badly betrayed me in the past. I had spent lavishly on each of them. It is a matter of great regret that I did not get anything from any of them in return. I shudder at the thought of my bitter experience. Now, with my hands folded, I most earnestly request you neither to ditch me nor to play with my life.

Nirdoshi, you are in the prime of your youth. You are intelligent, sagacious, well educated and mature enough to think over the matter in a calm, cool and objective manner, and to arrive at the best course for you to fellow. Please be free and frank, and tell me in the name of God whether you love me or not. I assure you that even if you do not love me, I shall not take it ill. On the contrary, I shall try my best to disappear from your life and to forget you for good. I shall never do anything to embarrass you or to hurt your tender feelings in any way.

I shall be highly obliged if you kindly speak the truth.

With deep love and best wishes,

Your devoted,

Vikram

(Full name and address of the recipient)

43. Reply to the above

(Full address of the writer, and date)

My dear Vikram,

I have just received your letter of the 4th instant. The contents of the letter have surprised me very much.

I am unable to understand why you have become suspicious of my bonafides in respect of my love for you. Know it for certain that I am neither cold nor indifferent to you. The fact is that you have gone astray in making an assessment of my attitude toward you. I love you from the innermost part of my heart. Do not worry about it any more.

I am very sorry to learn from your letter that many beautiful girls had betrayed you in the past. I am not like any of those unscrupulous girls who ditched you so badly. I shall never betray you. I am yours and I shall remain yours for ever.

I trust this makes everything quite clear to you.

With my profound love,

Your loving and devoted,

Nirdoshi

(Full name and address of the recipient)

44. Letter from a boy to a girl

(Full address of the writer, and date)

My dearest Nandini,

I have been suffering from a serious disease for many a day. Unfortunately, no medical practitioner can cure me of the disease. Let me give you the details of the disease. I love you most passionately but I did not disclose it to you out of fear. Now by the grace of God, the Greatest, I have summoned enough courage to pour out my heart to you. I love you to such an extent that no human soul can reach beyond it. In fact, I can not count all the ways I love you so dearly. We have known each other hardly for three months but it seems to me as if I have been in most intimate terms with you for a long span of three years.

Nandini, do you remember that it was at a marriage party where I first saw you. Please believe me when I say that I completely lost my heart to you then and there. It was certainly the love at first sight. Honestly speaking, I am very grateful to you because you also love me deeply. I am really a lucky person. When you meet and talk to me, I feel as if we have reached heaven.

I had always dreamt of a beautiful, graceful, slim, gay and smart girl. You fully fulfil all these qualifications. You are a tomboy (girl who enjoys rough noisy games). Besides, you are an extrovert (lively, cheerful and sociable person.) But at the same time, you are very well-mannered, well dressed, graceful in your gait (manner of walking) and sincere in what you say or do. Nandini darling, I like and love you to the fullest extent.

Not only that, even a prince, who is extremely charming and physically strong and stout, and a multi-millionaire, I would gladly and gratefully walk a distance of two kilometers on his knees in order to win your love, and to have you as his beloved and wife. I assure you I am not flattering you. What I am saying about you is nothing but a simple and pure truth. Nobody can challenge this statement of mine.

If you reciprocate my deep love, I shall certainly be the happiest man on the earth. Please believe me, whenever I think of you, it inevitably sweetens my soul with a heavenly bliss. You are the darling of my tender heart and you will remain so for ever. I have seen hundreds of young beautiful girls but none of them is even half so sweet and lovely as my Nandini darling.

I am most keenly awaiting your reply at the earlist.

Yours for ever,

Kuldip

(Full name and address of the recipient)

45. Reply from a beloved to her sweetheart

(Full address of the writer, and date)

Dear Govind,

I have just received your letter of the 13th instant in which you have, among other things, expressed your profound love for me. I thank you for it.

Really speaking, I had not even the slightest inkling of the fact that you would go so mad after my physical beauty, and so soon. My sincere and sound advice is that you should use your common sense and be patient. You must take all the relevant facts into due consideration before you take a final decision in the matter. It must be borne in mind that we have to go a long way.

Are you not aware of the old and wise saying that *discretion is the better part of valour* which still holds good? I want you to be fully guided by this tested and trusted dictum. Nothing should be done in a moment of rashness. You must not act rashly in such a delicate matter. Do you agree with me, Govind?

Let me tell you freely and frankly that I like you and I admire your intellectual ability and academic brilliance, but still I am not sure if I love you. It will definitely be wise and prudent on our part to go slow with much caution in our love affair. Otherwise we are bound to repent later on. You must not forget that life is not to be gambled away in a frenzy. I do admit that you are deeply attached to me but, so far as I am concerned, it is not at all the proper time for me to commit myself to anything. Let us have sufficient time to come close to each other more, to understand each other more. We must always remember that the path of love is strewn with both roses and thorns. Let us not choose thorns, instead of roses, in haste. It is too early to take a final decision now.

Let me tell you something of paramount (Supreme) importance to you. My be, you come across a girl who is much more attractive, intelligent and educated than I. Today you are burning with passionate love for me, and tomorrow some other girl may heat you more intensely. She may be than to you what I am now. So, please have patience. It is so easy to begin, but so difficult to sustain it. It is better to delay the matter than to stoop to fully in haste, and then to repent at leisure.

Yours,

Kusum

(Full name and address of the recipient)

46. Love letter from a Professor to one of his girl students

(Full address of the writer, and date)

My dear Champa,

I am sure you will be totally surprised to receive this letter. Let me frankly tell you that I began loving you ever since I met you while taking your class about a month ago. I have completely lost my heart and soul to you. Although you are not a paragon of beauty, I still love you most passionately. The reason is not far to seek. You are soft-spoken, smart and intelligent. Your beauty lies not only in your physique but also in your brain. Your attentiveness in the class and the manner in which you reply to my questions are indeed a matter of pride.

Whenever I think of your glowing youth my tender heart is filled with tremendous pleasure. Champa, believe me, I have gone almost mad. I can never think of anything else. I yearn to get closer to you and know more about you. In you I am sure to find the woman who fits my idea of beauty and genius. I sincerely wish to love you and be loved by you. I hope you undertand.

You have nothing to fear from me. I assure you I shall never do anything indecent, lewd or improper to tarnish your or my reputation. So I most earnestly request you to allow me to meet you for some time after the college hours. Give me a chance to prove my love for you.

I shall be most grateful if you very kindly spare your precious time to make me happy.

Yours ever,

Prem Nath

(Full name and address of the recipient)

47. Reply to the above

(Full address of the writer, and date)

Dear Professor,

Know it for certain that your letter of the 2nd instant has not surprised me even in the least. It is a fact that almost all men are like you. They run after girls and young women. Such a man wants to possess only the body of a woman.

In your letter you have tried to divert my attention from your lewd intentions to my intelligence and so on and so forth. But I shall never allow you to befool me by means of flattery. I am astonished at the fact that you have not even paid attention to the age difference.

So whatever it is, I do not want to pursue the matter further and I severely warn you not to write or talk to me in future otherwise I will report the matter to the higher authorities.

Your student,

Champa

(Full name and address of the recipient)

48. Love letter from a neighbour to a young married woman

(Full address of the writer, and date)

Dearest Sonali,

Your name is very sweet. It gladdens my heart to a very great extent. I am lucky to have plenty of opportunities of seeing you day and night. I feel the craving (strong desire) in the inner-most part of my tender heart and though as far as norms of the society are concerned it might be wrong but still my heart is full of genuine and passionate love for you. You have become my heart and soul.

Sonali, do you know that the stolen glimpses of a woman's body when the woman is totally unaware of the observer are sweet? I very much enjoy looking at your attractive body whenever possible and few days earlier when I saw you standing before the mirror in your bathing gown, you were looking fabulous. I have since then been dreaming of you day and night. I still vividly (clearly) remember how you frowned and smiled, and even made faces at your own image in the mirror in order to see in which particular fashion you looked most attractive and charming.

Sonali, I shall be most grateful if you very kindly give me a chance to meet and talk with you for a while so as to satisfy my eagerness.

I am keenly awaiting your early and affirmative reply.

Yours for ever,

Sundar Lal

(Full name and address of the recipient)

49. Love letter from a college student to a poor school girl who sells flowers

(Full address of the writer, and date)

My dear Nutan,

I know it very well that you do not think of me or my pure and true love for you. Perhaps, the reason is that you are just like one of those little flowers which you carry on your head every day. Nutan, are you aware of the fact that your tiny lips are just like the petals of the sweet flowers which people buy from you for the worship of their gods or for making garlands for thier beloveds? I have closely observed that your eyes twinkle like the buds of the flowers which glisten (shine brightly) with the dew drops in your little basket.

I think of you every night while going to bed. I keep waiting for you at my window every morning. When you appear before the window, I always make some excuse to detain you in order that I can look at your sweet, lovely, innocent face for a longer time. But you never think of me, not because you do not like me but because you are yet too young to think of man on his love. I love you very dearly. Why do I love you? I love you merely for your innocence. When you will grow up, you will lose your innocence and you will certainly blush and hesitate to talk to, or appear before, me.

I earnestly request you to reciprocate my love.

Your early and favourable reply will highly oblige me.

Yours for ever,

Mohan

(Full name and address of the recipient)

50. Reply to the above

(Full address of the writer, and date)

My dear Mohan,

Your letter of the 13th instant has gladdened me most.

First, let me assure you that you are a god to me.

I cannot aspire to love you, I can simply worship you with deep devotion and dedication. Please bear it in mind that I am not so tiny as you have taken me to be. I fully understand everything. I also feel that I have a body, a heart and a soul. As ill luck would have it (unfortunately), my parents are poor. This is why I have to sell flowers in order to meet my school expenses and augment the family income. It is my good fortune that you love me so dearly. Nobody else ever cared to notice me.

People say that the rich hate the poor. Your parents are rich. So I am terribly afraid of them. You will also hate me when you marry a rich girl. She will look much more beautiful than myself in your eyes. She will wear fine clothes and dear (expensive) ornaments. On the other hand, I wear only dirty rags (old, worn or torn clothes). Do you still love me?

I must not try to catch the moon. After you will have married, I shall, as usual, sell flowers to you. I shall also make garlands for your pretty wife to look prettier in your eyes. Every day I shall come to you with the same basket of flowers. Tell me honestly, whether you will buy flowers from at me then in the same manner as you do now.

Mohan, I do not want anything from you but I want you to marry a beautiful girl whom I can adorn with all the flowers in my basket. This is the best thing for you to do in the existing circumstances.

Yours sincerely,

Nutan

(Full name and address of the recipient)

51. Love letter from a customer to a European waitress in a restaurant

(Full address of the writer, and date)

Dearest Diana,

You are already well aware of the fact that love is not confined to any nationality or race. I am sure you will not mind that I happen to be an Indian. I am a man and you are a girl. That is all we should, know. Let me tell you at the very outset that I love you deeply. You may like to know why I have taken a fancy for you when I can get so many Indian girls. Honestly speaking, I dislike our Indian girls because I hate their manner of dress and ways. They are unusually shy and timid. If a man goes to kiss a girl, she closes her eyes and shrug her shoulders as if she is going to faint. But European girls are not like that. They are bold, forward and sprightly.

I have taken a fancy for you simply because you are so smart, sprightly and forward. Whenever I happened to visit your restaurant, I noticed that you looked trim and smart with your frock on. I am sure, when I shall kiss you, you will not timidly close your eyes and shrug your shoulders to avoid the kiss, but on the other hand, you will clasp me with your arms twining your neck with mine and try to dissolve my entire body into yours and your entire body into mine.

I am also highly impressed by your gait. You walk proudly as if you are conscious of your immortal treasures. I don't say Indian girls are not attractive but most of them don't know how to maintain their treasures. You know how to talk, how to smile, how to walk, how to sit and how to receive all the caresses from a lover.

sweetened my tender heart beyond expression in language.

Today I must tell you that I feel extremely thrilled when I get your letters. Your pure and deep love really creates tremendous mental peace and physical strength and stamina in me. You are my goddess. You have asked me to define my love for you. Very well, let me express it here. Know it for certain that my deepest love for you can neither be defined nor explained in words. It can never be bound by definitions or words in any language in the world. It has a centre but no circumference. You are the centre. I love you just the way you are.

Your letters are the pills of boundless energy for me. Darling, I love you most passionately. I know you also love me from the bottom of your heart. In other words, you love me as passionately as I love you. Am I right Dropti darling? Even if you grow old you will remain young and beautiful for me as you are now. I shall continue to love you most dearly and honestly from the depth of my heart till the moment I die. To me life without you is meaningless.

I hope you got your answer just the way you wanted. Please reply at once.

Yours own,

Damodar

(Full name and address of the recipient)

67. Love letter from a young man to a lady who travelled in a train

(Full address of the writer, and date)

Dear Namita,

What a wonderful journey we together had! It was a chance meeting on the platform. The train was late. I was alone and feeling bored. Then you appeared on the scene like a bright sunshine after gloom. You politely enquired about the train and then I offered you my company. We talked on so many pleasant things. We had our coffee in the refreshment room. Thereafter the train arrived and we travelled together. I liked you, and my liking grew into pure and deep love within that short span of four hours. You reciprocated my love with a charming smile. I hope you will kindly and surely agree with me that it was an entirely unforgettable experience. It was indisputably a very memorable journey.

Kindly believe me when I say that your fascinating and beautiful image has been deeply imprinted on my heart. It can never be removed. Shall I be ever so fortunate as to have you as my life partner and companion? My love for you is so deep that I cannot express it in words. Honestly speaking, I do not find adequate words to convey my deep sense of attachment and passion for you.

Namita, I am at my wits end (confused), thirsty and all afire (on fire). Only you can guide me, quench my thirst and extinguish this consuming fire. I want you to be my guiding star, send the showers of your love to save me from desperation.

You obliged me by giving your sweet company and favourable response. You gave me your photograph at parting, and I am so grateful to you for all this. I love you and want to be loved by you.

Your early and favourable reply will surely and fully oblige me.

Yours for ever,

Manohar

(Full name and address of the recipient)

68. A married man falls in love with his wife's younger sister

(Full address of the writer, and date)

My dear Supriya,

People say that a love affair with a sister-in-law is sweet. So nobody should marry a girl who has no younger sister.

I never met you before my marriage. Otherwise I would have definitely chosen you as my wife, instead of your elder sister. Because you are younger and more tempting and sprightly in your manners than your elder sister. You are naughty and mischievous. You do not easily yield to my tricks. Many times, you shipped out of my grasp whenever I wanted to hold you in my arms. There were also some occasions when I failed to kiss you. Many times, you ran out of one room into another whenever I happened to chase you. Sometimes I seemed to catch hold of the end of your saree, but then, you quickly released your saree from my fingers only to leave me gasping with unfulfilled hankerings.

Your naughty smiles at my failures to catch you are most alluring. They madden me to chase you and to pounce upon you with a stronger desire. I love you because you know the art of tempting and capturing the heart of a man. I love your smiles, your frowns, your blushes, your beautiful face, your splendid figure, your pinches, and even your bites and scratches on my arms.

I most ardently request you to reciprocate my love for you.

I am waiting with bated breath for your early and favourable reply.

Yours,

Avinash

(Full name and address of the recipient)

69. Love letter from a stepmother-in-law to her stepson-in-law

(Fill address of the writer, and date)

My dear Gajanand,

I am sure you will be totally surprised to read the contents of this letter of mine .

I have been tryir g to suppress my heart for a long time. In the eyes of the people, I am your mother-in-law and you are my son-in-law.

But the fact is tha: your wife is not my own daughter. Thus you are not my own son-in-law. Your wife is nearest in blood to my husband, and not to me. It is, therefore, not a crime on my part if I say that I love you. I, as an ordinary woman, but not as your mother-in-law, love you. Let me make it more clear. I do not love my husband at all, but I love you passionately. How can I love my husband who is as old as my father ? He has married me not for my love, but for the sake of my body.

Gajanand, am I not more intelligent, beautiful and educated than the woman you have married? To speak the truth, I never treated you as my son-in-law. I always treated you in the way a young woman should treat a healthy and handsome young man. I want you never to think even for a moment that I am a woman of loose character. I am as virtuous as your wife. My only misfortune is that I am married to an old and weak man who is entirely unfit for me.

Darling, I do not want to rob your wife of your love; I do not want to deprive her of her rightful shelter in your bosom. But you must grant me also some little corner in your heart. I do not think it is too great a demand on my part.

I am awaiting your favourable reply.

Yours,

Sita

(Full name and address of the recipient)

70. Reply to the above

(Full address of the writer, and date)

My dear mother-in-law,

Your letter has really surprised me to a great extent . But I cannot blame you much for what you have penned in the letter. If I were in the same situation, I would have done the same thing. I have full sympathy for you. I am sorry to say that you have to obey social customs, traditions, and so on. You cannot disobey or ignore them. There is no remedy for your misfortune.

I can well realise how difficult it is for you to be reconciled to an old and emaciated husband from day to day, from week to week, from month to month, and from year to year. I can well imagine the burning desires of your heart which have been consuming your body and soul. If I were not related to you as your son-in-law, I would have surely gone out of my way to quench at least some of your legitimate hankerings.

All that I can do at present is to solemnly pray to God, the Greatest, so that he may grant you peace of mind, and solve your problem.

Your son-in-law,

Gajanand

(Full name and address of the recipient)

71. *Love letter from a rich and highly educated woman to an ordinary soldier in the army*

(Full address of the writer, and date)

My dear Bir Bahadur,

I know fully well that this letter of mine will surely surprise you to a very great extent.

You may wonder how a woman of my education and social status can ever fall in love with an ordinary soldier like you. But you must know that love is blind. None can deny the fact that common soldiers like you fight and die in the battlefield for the defence of the motherland.

Bir Bahadur, I love you for many reasons. I love you because you are strong and stout, brave and handsome. You rarely come in touch with women. How can a young person like you decide to live a bachelor's life? Or is it that no girl has as yet expressed her love for you? Believe me, my love for you is true and I shall consider myself the luckiest girl on earth if you will reciprocate my love for you.

I am eagerly awaiting your favourable reply at the earliest.

Yours,

Savita

(Full name and address of the recipient)

72. Love letter from a young man to his cousin sister

(Full address of the writer, and date)

My dear Meetu,

We have done nothing wrong. But the world says that there is something wrong between you and me. The world is nothing but a set of malicious fools. Never care for such a world. I know that my love for you is absolutely pure. Love is neither a crime nor a sin. We have been bred and brought up together for over twenty years. We cannot hate each other. We will always love each other. No power on earth, not even death, can separate us.

If the world says that a man has no right to love his cousin sister, to admire her beauty, to worship her sometimes as an angel, I shall certainly spurn that world in the way I spurn the dogs in the streets. In am my own master. I am a breaker of illogical social conventions. I must adore you in my heart of hearts. I must hold you even in my arms and pull you close to me with deepest affections. Let the world stare at both of us.

You are not my real sister. Our parents are different. It does not matter if our parents do not agree to our sincere proposal. We have nothing to be afraid of. Both of us are well educated. We can earn enough to live a decent and independent life. It is money alone that matters in the world. With money you can buy power, position, reputation, name, fame, influence, and so on.

I cannot live without you. Believe me, I never think even in my dream that I am your cousin . I feel that I am a young man and you are a young woman. So we have every right to love and marry each other. Whatever may be the case, I must marry you. It is totally impossible for me to live without you. Let the whole world come in between us, and yet I must have you as my wife. I want to cease to be your cousin. I want to be your husband for ever. I know you will also want to be my wife.

I do hope you will make it convenient to send me a favourable reply as soon as possible.

Yours,

Madhav

(Full name and address of the recipient)

73. Reply to the above

(Full address of the writer, and date)

My dear Madhav,

I have just got your affectionate letter. I thank you very deeply for it.

At the very outset, let me tell you frankly that I highly appreciate your deep love for me. At the same time I am very sorry to say that I cannot appreciate your arguments in defence of marriage between cousins. In my opinion, blood relation must be honoured. Otherwise, the future generation of the human race will degenerate both physically and intellectually. This is a biological truth.

I can never agree to marry you. I shall always love you as my dearest brother. You should bear it in mind that a sister can love her cousin brother more than a wife can love her husband.

You must also remember that love between the husband and the wife may simply be a desire of the flesh. On the other hand, love between a brother and a sister is a sublime hankering of the soul. If you really love, you can definitely love me as your sister.

Your affectionate sister,

Meetu

(Full name and address of the recipient)

74. Love letter from a famous maestro to a beautiful blind girl

(Full address of the writer, and date)

My dear Kalpana,

Please do not be surprised to receive this letter.

You have never seen me. Perhaps you have heard my voice. I am extremely sorry that you have been robbed of your light when you are the light of the world. God must have given eyes to your heart in order to enable you to see me. I am sure you can see me with the light of your heart. So it does not matter if there is no light in your eyes. Only those who have no eyes of the heart require the light of the eyes to see things where there is darkness.

Kalpana, I have seen you innumerable times. I have minutely observed that when you walk, you do not grope with your fingers as any other blind man gropes in the light or we grope in the dark. When you stand before me, you blush as if you can see how I keep on gazing at you. Can you really see everything around you? Otherwise how can you be so sensitive to every stare, every breath, and every approaching shadow of a man?

Please believe me when I say that I love you very dearly. My love for you is pure and true. I shall always do my best to make you happy and cheerful.

I shall be very glad to receive a line in reply, stating that you reciprocate my love.

Yours,

Anil

(Full name and address of the recipient)

75. Reply to the above

(Full address of the writer, and date)

Dearest Anil,

I have just received your sweet letter. I thank you most profoundly for it.

You have given me my eyes. But in the eyes of the world, I have no eyes. Through the eyes of my heart, I have seen you many a time. You are handsome, noble, gracious, kind-hearted and sympathetic. You have a very sweet voice. Am I worthy of your love? Anil darling, hold out your hands, I want to feel your touch.

God, the Greatest, is very kind to me. He has sent you to me. Let not other people stare at me. Let not the world think of me or to feel for me. You alone can do all such things. You can lend me light. Your words will be my light. So long, the whole world was blank and dark and I felt as if I was all alone in this vast world. Anil, do you really love me? Do I look beautiful and attractive to you? Every woman is proud of her beauty. Can you hear the beating of my heart? My tender heart beats for you. I want you to possess me in every way. I love you passionately, as much as you love me.

Anil, I have everything which any other woman possesses or which a man desires. Let me feel you with my arms and with my pink lips. It is a tremendous joy for a young woman to lie in the bosom of a young and healthy man. Will you really shelter me in your bosom?

I am most eager to meet you at the earliest. Please tell me where and when I can see you.

Yours for ever,

Kalpana

(Full name and address of the recipient)

76. *Love letter from a tutor to the mother of one of his pupils*

(Full address of the writer, and date)

Dear Mrs. Gita,

You will perhaps be totally taken aback to receive this letter, because I happen to be the tutor of your two little daughters.

Please do not think that I am both ambitious and impertinent. I cannot forget that I am a young man and you are a beautiful and attractive woman. It goes without saying that I am much younger to you in age. But we must not forget that love is blind, and that everything is fair in war and love. Pure love has nothing to do with age, physical appearance, complexion, parentage, and so on. To speak the truth, I had fallen in deep love with you on the first day of my visit to your place. You often used to sit by the side of your children to see how I coach them. Your stunning beauty has completely charmed me. I cannot think of any other girl or woman. So far I had no chance to meet such a beauty.

I am in the know of the fact that your husband is a very rich man. But you must remember that I am young and strong and stout, well educated, polite and polished in manners, well informed of men and matters and endowed with intellectual ability.

I do not want you to leave your husband and children. Though I love you I shall never marry you. You must lead your usual life with your husband and children. I entreat you to kindly permit me only to love you. I am not interested in anything else.

I shall be most grateful if you very kindly make it convenient to meet me only once a week at a place of your own choice.

I am most keenly awaiting your early and favourable reply.

Yours,

Sunil

(Full name and address of the recipient)

77. Reply to the above

(Full address of the writer, and date)

Dear Mr. Sunil

Your letter of the 13th instant has completely shocked and surprised me. I never expected such a nasty letter from you.

It is a fact that, in general, every woman feels flattered when she is highly admired and deeply loved by a man who is young, well educated, healthy and handsome. But I can never forget the fact that I am the wife of your master. You are a mere private teacher of our children. You must always remember that a tutor is nothing but a glorified domestic servant.

I know you have been attracted by my extra ordinary beauty. You have indirectly hinted that I am an old woman. Let me tell you that you are wholly mistaken. I am not at all old. As a matter of fact I am just a few years elder to you.

I cannot encourage you even as my admirer. The reason is not far to seek. I live with my devoted and dear husband, and lovely children. It will certainly be a sin on my part to think of any other man. You have disturbed my heart and soul. You amply deserve to be punished for your unlawful and undesirable hankering. From tomorrow, you must stop coming to our house. You must not try to see my children in future. Otherwise you will find yourself in hot waters.

Yours sincerely,

Mrs. Gita

(Full name and address of the recipient)

78. Love letter from a girl to a boy

(Full address of the writer, and date)

My dear Atul,

It is already well known to you that generally boys write love-letters to girls. But here the case is quite the opposite. A girl pens a love-letter to a boy with whom she has fallen in deep love. This clearly and fully shows my passionate love for you. Is it not? I do hope you fully agree with me on this. Please treat me as your true and devoted darling.

Atul, please believe me when I say that I have always been thinking of you ever since I met you ten months ago at the birthday party of Pramila who is one of my bosom friends since my childhood. Now it seems to me as if a long span of ten years has gone by since then. This unmistakably means that you have charmed me to a very great extent. I cannot concentrate on anything else, despite my best efforts. I always think of you. I want to be with you every moment.

Do you remember that I proposed to you, and you solemnly promised to marry me after having consultation with your parents? You did not bother to write me a letter or to meet me for so many days. This fact has pained me much. I never expected it from you. I do not know what prevented you from contacting me personally, on the phone or by writing. So I am extremely anxious about your welfare.

I am most keenly awaiting your early reply in detail.

With deepest love,

Yours for ever,

Shilpa

(Full name and address of the recipient)

79. Reply to the above

(Full address of the writer, and date.)

My dear Shilpa,

I have just received your sweet letter. The contents of the letter have filled my heart with genuine pleasure. So I hasten to thank you from the bottom of my tender heart. I am extremely sorry that I could not contact you for so many days for reasons beyond my control. I entreat you to excuse me for the inordinate delay on my part. Such a delay will not be repeated in future.

I have discussed the matter with mother. I have told her everything about you in detail. She has kindly agreed to the proposal. Father is out of station. He is expected back by the15th of this month. Thereafter, it will be finally decided. Let us solemnly pray to god to help us in this regard.

Tell your parents about it. Let me know their reactions as soon as possible.

Will you kindly take the trouble to send me an immediate reply in detail?

Yours for ever,

Atul

(Full name and address of the recipient)

80. Reply to the above reply

(Full address of the writer, and date)

My dear Atul,

I received your letter this forenoon. The contents of the

letter have gladdened me beyond expression in language. To speak the truth, I expected what you have written. Heart and soul, I pray to God, the greatest, to unite both of us in wedlock, and to grant us happiness, prosperity and peaceful married life.

Father and mother have read your letter. They have no objection to our early marriage. Father will write to your father in this connection. You must inform me as soon as your father returns home.

I keenly desire to meet you any day convenient to you. The earlier, the better. I leave the college at 4-30 p.m. daily. You may come and meet me outside the main gate of the college.

I hope this finds you in the best of spirits.

Yours,

Shilpa

(Full name and address of the recipient)

81. A man falls in love with a woman ballet dancer

(Full address of the writer, and date)

My dear Indira,

I am one of your great admirers. The lustre of your eyes enthralled me when I saw your lovely dance last night. Honestly speaking, the rhythm of your movement had charmed me beyond expression in language. You are so beautiful and attractive. I have never seen such a woman in my life.

Indira, please believe me, I had fallen in love with you as soon as you began to dance. I must call you the apple of my eyes. I do not want to hide anything from you. I am already married.

Unfortunately, my wife is very ugly. She is very fat. She is as black as coal. Her voice is harsh. We have been married for a little over four years but we have not yet been blessed with a child. I have been living an unhappy married life.

She has gone to her parents. She will stay with them for one month. I have filed for divorce and hope to be a free man in another six months time. I request you to visit me and I shall do my best for your comfortable stay. Even a day spent in your desired company will please me beyond measure.

Should I wait for you? If so, where and when? I do hope you will not disappoint me.

yours,

Aman

(Full name and address of the recipient)

82. Reply to the above

(Full address of the writer, and date)

Dear Mr. Aman,

I was totally surprised to receive your letter. How did you dare to write such a nasty letter to me? What do you take me for?

You are a married man. You are fed up with your fat and ugly wife. I have not so far experienced marital bliss. It is most shocking that you intend to rob me of the flower of chastity. I can never think of such a thing. You are a devil of the worst type in the garb of a man.

You must keep up your promises made to your wife on the eve of your marriage. Do your best to make her happy. Never think of other woman. You must not try to lead a lustful life. You must be fully faithful to your wife. Maybe your lustful intentions are causing disharmony in your married life. Improve on your intentions instead of divorcing your wife. She may certainly not be as ugly as you have described her. Your justifications do not please me.

Do not ever write to me or try to contact me again.

Yours sincerely,

Indira

(Full name and address of the recipient)

83. Love letter from a young man to a girl

(Full address of the writer, and date)

My dear Kunti,

Perhaps you will rub your eyes in utter surprise to receive this letter from one whom you might have fully forgotten.

Let me remind you that we happened to meet each other in the train from Agra to New Delhi about three weeks ago. We sat side by side. We had a really pleasant talk during the journey. And I had the good fortune of having tea with you. You were kind enough to give me your address. I had all along been thinking of writing to you but one thing or another always stood in the way. That was why I could not write to you earlier, despite my best longing.

Here I deem it apt to be frank and to pour out my true and profound love for you. I earnestly request you not to get angry with me. I have keenly been looking forward to meeting you as early as possible at a place and time to be chosen by you.

Will you be kind enough to send me an early reply?

With deep love,

Yours for ever,

Rohit

(Full name and address of the recipient)

84. Reply to the above

(Full address of the writer, and date)

Dear Mr. Rohit,

Yesterday I received your letter of the 4th instant. I was totally surprised to read the contents of the letter. You should not have penned the letter at all.

I very much regret to say that I shall never be available for such a meeting. My parents are of orthodox views. Naturally they are averse to any such meeting. Honestly speaking, I also cherish those views in such matters.

You are, therefore, requested neither to write to, nor to try to meet, me in future.

Yours sincerely,

Kunti

(Full name and address of the recipient)

85. Another reply

(Full address of the writer, and date)

My dear Rohit,

I have just got your lovely letter. I am entirely enthralled to read the contents of the letter. I have already read the letter twice. I shall read it again. I am happy to know you have not forgotten me.

The fact that you love me profoundly, has gladdened me much. Rohit, please believe me, I do not find adequate words in language to express the depth of my delight. You will be beside yourself with joy to know that I also love you, but only to some extent. Right now, I cannot and must not love you deeply. The reason is that I want to know you more. I cannot love you deeply unless I know you thoroughly. Let us wait and see how things shape up with the passage of time.

I sincerely advise you to beware. You must always bear it in mind that the road is not so clear as you think. It is strewn with thorns. We must tread cautiously. Let us be slow but steady. Let us wait and watch. We must be cautious. We must not jump into the abyss so as to be lost for ever.

Let us meet on Saturday, the 9th instant at 3-30 p.m. at the bus-stop outside my college gate. Thence (from there) we shall visit a good restaurant where we can have a tete-a-tete over a cup of tea. I must leave you at 5-30 p.m. positively, in order to reach home at or before 6-30 p.m. So you must not try to detain me beyond 5-30 p.m.

With profound love,

Yours,

Kunti

(Full name and address of the recipient)

86. Love letter from a young man to a girl beggar

(Full address of the writer, and date)

My dear Sumitra,

Let me be fully free and frank with you. You are dressed in rags and tatters. You are a beggar by profession. You are earning your livelihood by begging. Do not take offence to my saying so. But I am very glad that you look so beautiful and attractive. Believe me, I could never imagine before I had seen you that a girl can look so beautiful and alluring even in tatters. Normally every human eye is attracted by fine and costly clothes, fashionable style of dressing, and bright jewellery, etc. But now I find that clothes, jewellery, and so on, are absolutely useless for a form which is lovely by nature. You are a shining example in this regard. It is a fact that a person who has no eye for the real form and shape of the perfect feminity always tries to search for beauty in the clothes, ornaments, and so forth.

It is already well known to you that people generally turn away beggars simply because they wear dirty and torn clothes. In my considered opinion, such people are fools. If you wear fine clothes, good jewellery and cosmetics which the rich and fashionable women daily use, you will, I am sure look like a princess, and the rich and fashionable women, will look like owls. There are women in many of the rich and educated families, who, even with all their decorations, look like maidservants.

Sumitra, I have really fallen in deep love with you, not because you are a paragon of beauty, but because you are very poor and yet you wear a smile on your face. The fact that you go unnoticed, uncared and undefended in this vast world has greatly influenced me to love you dearly. I never like to look at those women who are proud of their wealth, social status, and so on. I assure you I shall love you till the last moment of my life.

I shall be glad to receive a line in reply from you as early as possible.

Yours for ever,

Raghav

(Full name and address of the recipient)

87. Reply to the above

(Full address of the writer, and date)

My dear Raghav,

I have just got your wonderful letter. The contents of the letter have filled my heart with joy. I do not find adequate words in language to express the depth of my boundless delight and gratitude.

To speak the truth, you have done me the greatest honour by saying that you really love me and that you will continue to love me till the last moment of your life.

Let me assure you that I fully agree to be your beloved. I shall also love you most dearly. I shall serve you to the best of my ability. I shall always do everything to please you.

Let us meet on Tuesday, the 14th instant at about 4-30 p.m. outside the main gate of the Government Hospital. You must await me till I come.

Heart and soul, I pray to God to grant you a long life replete with wealth, fame and glory, verve and vim, happiness and sound health.

Your devoted,

Sumitra

(Full name and address of the recipient)

88. Love letter from a fiance to his betrothed

(Full address of the writer, and date)

My dear Sudesh,

The 4th April is certainly a great day for both of us. Do you remember that it was on that auspicious day when we met each other for the first time? The first moment of our meeting was excessively exciting. Do you agree with me on this? We must not forget that moment. Is it not, Sudesh?

Kindly believe me, I still feel the soft touch of your long, lovely and finely shaped fingers which I experienced while I slipped the diamond ring on to your finger. My eyes were glued for a few moments to your rosy cheeks and pink lips. Those momentous moments will always finger in my memory, and keep the flame of deep love burning bright in my tender heart for ever.

It is a matter of great joy to think that we will be united in wedlock after twenty days, and you will be mine for ever. To speak the truth, this very thought fills my heart with tremendous delight. It will indubitably be a great joy to be your husband. I assure you from the bottom of my heart that I shall continue to love you till the last moment of my life . I shall fully satisfy you in every aspect. You will never have an occasion to complain against me. All your needs will be wholly met to your entire satisfaction.

Darling, you cannot realise how much passionate I have become to kiss and embrace you. I think of you every moment.

I hope this finds you all at home in the best of health and happiness.

Please reply as soon as possible.

With deepest love,

Yours for ever,

Bhim

(Full name and address of the recipient)

89. Love letter from a college student to his class-mate

(Full address of the writer, and date)

Dearest Anjali,

First I want you not to be taken aback to receive this letter.

You will remember that we have been together as class-mates in the college for about two years. Let me be free and frank to tell you that you attracted me from the very beginning, and I liked you much from the core of my heart. I must speak the truth. This liking has gradually developed into a great attachment for you.

The pure and simple truth is that I am in most profound love with you. The depth of my love for you really beggars description in language.

It is my firm belief that you have a soft corner for me. However, you have always been trying to hide it. It is but natural for a girl who is shy by nature. It became clear to me on the occasion of our college excursion in the recent past. You have always been polite, nice and considerate to me. For so long, I could not muster enough courage to tell you all this. I love you so much that I cannot think of anything else. Your stunning beauty has been haunting me day and night.

Anjali, please believe me when I say that I need you to survive. I cannot live without you. You are my guiding star and angel.

I entreat you to reciprocate my love.

I am keenly awaiting your early reply.

With deepest love,

Yours for ever,

Gopal

(Full name and address of the recipient)

90. A boy writes a love letter to a girl

(Full address of the writer, and date)

My dear Malti,

Do you know that I love you very passionately? Really speaking, I cannot count all the ways I love you. Perhaps you will remember that we have so far met each other only twice, but it seems to me as if I have been in love with you for two years.

It was at the birthday party of a friend of mine about three months ago that I first saw you. I lost my heart to you then and there. Truly speaking, it was love at first sight. Know it for certain that love at first sight is the best love. So I earnestly request you to treat me as your best lover in every aspect. I solemnly swear that I shall love you very dearly till the last moment of my life. I am fully prepared to walk on my knees a distance of a kilometre at a stretch as a proof of my pure and boundless love for you, and to have you as my beloved.

Malti darling, if you reciprocate my love, I shall be happy beyond expression in language. I shall gladly do everything to please you and to make you happy for ever.

Kindly make it convenient to send me a reply as soon as possible.

Yours for ever,

Mukesh

(Full name and address of the recipient)

91. Love letter from a whore's daughter to her mother's client

(Full address of the writer, and date)

My dear Rameshwar,

It is my firm belief that you love me very much. This is why you make frequent visits to my mother in order to have chance meetings with me. It has been observed that you heap costly gifts, and large amounts of money on her merely for my sake.

Let me tell you freely and frankly that it is my bad luck that I happen to be a prostitute's daughter. To speak the truth, I vehemently hate this profession. After a year or so, mother will surely force me into this shameful and detestable (hateful) profession. There is no doubt even in the least that she loves me. But her love for money really baffles expression in language. It is but natural for a whore to earn as much money as possible. Rameshwar, you are my true and passionate lover. I assure you I also love you very deeply. Now I want you to marry me as early as possible, so that I may be able to live a respectable life as your wife.

You are a great and grand person. Perhaps, God has sent you here to rescue me from this brothel. I shall commit suicide if you do not marry me. I am fully prepared to face any danger, provided you assure me of your love and protection. I have finally chosen you as my husband and lover.

I have complete faith in you. I shall remain most grateful and devoted to you till the last moment of my life.

Yours,

Ritu

(Full name and address of the recipient)

92. Love letter from a lecturer to a lady lecturer in a college

(Full address of the writer, and date)

My dear Divya,

You are already well aware of the fact that I have deep love for you. This love has turned into an intense love-sickness. I feel sowewhat mentally disturbed. Consequently, I have become very listless. That was why I could not attend the college for six days. Honestly speaking, I was expecting a visit from you, but in vain. Dearest, I hope you are hale and hearty.

I know you also love me dearly. I am keen to have you in my arms. The warm and hard touch of your beautiful body will surely give me tremendous pleasure.

Why don't you come and encircle me like a flowering creeper? I always think of you. I want you to come, and to embrace and kiss me as you once did in the not so distant past.

I have grown very weak. I shall not survive without you. Please come and help me. Do not leave me reeling under the load of passionate love for you. Know it for certain that my love has grown deeper and deeper with your somewhat favourable response.

I assure you I love you very deeply very sincerely and very passionately.

Will you kindly make it convenient to send me a line in reply as soon as possible ?

With deepest love,

Yours for ever,

Monu

(Full name and address of the recipient)

93. Love letter from a school girl to a boy

(Full address of the writer, and date)

Dear Kailash,

I am sure you will be both surprised and flattered to receive this love-letter of mine. This is my first letter to a boy. Really speaking, I love and like you very much. This is why I am writing this letter to express my pure love for you.

You are innocent, handsome, healthy and wealthy. You have an attractive personality. All this has encouraged me to pen this letter. I wonder if you ever think of me. I always think of you. I highly admire your sweet and mild voice and graceful manners.

I find that there is an invitation for intimacy in your suggestive smiles and gestures. You are always on the look-out for an opportunity to talk to me, but your shyness is a hindrance. Now this love-letter of mine will certainly embolden you to come closer.

I assure you nobody knows anything about my love for you. Even if it is known, I do not care, provided you love me. I tell you from the bottom of my heart that if you reciprocate my love, I shall be happy beyond expression in language. In case, you do not accept my love, please forgive me and forget the matter for ever.

I am keenly awaiting your early reply.

With most profound love,

Yours,

Kanta

(Full name and address of the recipient)

94. Reply to the above

(Full address of the writer, and date)

My dear Kanta

I have just received your sweet letter. The contents of the letter have filled my tender heart with genuine pleasure. I thank you most profoundly for it.

Kanta, please believe me, I do not find adequate words in language to express the depth of my gratitude to you. You have saved me from a bewilderment. Now I feel immensely relieved of a burden which was lying heavy on my heart. To be frank, I totally failed to rise to the occasion to clearly express my deep and sincere love for you. However, I was in search of an opportunity to tell you all about my tender feelings for you.

I am a boy and you are a girl. I lack the courage, and you possess it so abundantly. I very highly admire you for it.

You are so lovely, so nice, so sweet, so intelligent, so lovable and so co-operative. Please take it for granted that I love you most dearly. I think of you every moment. I shall always do everything for your happiness till the last moment of my life.

I shall wait for you at the bus-stand outside the gate of your school on Friday, the 8th instant, at 1-30 p.m. Even if you are late, I shall certainly await you till you come. You have nothing to worry about it.

With profound love,

Yours,

Kailash

(Full name and address of the recipient)

95. Love letter from a lady to her lover

(Full address of the writer, and date)

Dearest Mahesh,

You must always remember that I love you and your lovely letters that you send occasionally. Yesterday it was very cold and cloudy.

But for me, it was all sunshine and pleasant, because I received another love letter from you.

Mahesh dear, you are always in my heart. I think of you every moment. Even when I sleep, you appear in my dreams. I read and re-read your every letter. I have read your recent letter seven times. Every reading had given me tremendous pleasure. Every time I found something more interesting, refreshing and invigorating. While going through the letter, I felt as if you were talking with me here.

Please take care of your health in these days of cold wave.

Yours lovingly,

Meena

(Full name and address of the recipient)

96. Love letter from a boy to a girl studying in a college

(Full address of the writer, and date)

My dear Bina,

I had occasions to meet you many a time. But I never

observed that you were such a treasure. Somehow I failed to take note of your exceptional beauty all these days. Yesterday when I saw you coming up the staircase, I was stunned by your gorgeous looks.

I entreat you for your intimacy. Will you kindly allow me to visit you at your residence, off and on ? I shall help you in preparing your lessons, and so on. In case, you do not like my visiting you at your home, I can meet you outside the Hanuman Temple every Tuesday at about 5-30 p.m. or so.

I shall be glad to serve you in any way you like. Now it is for you to decide how to make use of my services.

Your early reply will highly oblige me.

Yours,

Madan

(Full name and address of the recipient)

97. Reply to the above

(Full address of the writer, and date)

Dear Madan,

Yesterday I received your letter of the 2nd instant.

I am sorry to say that I cannot allow you to visit me at our residence even occasionally. My parents are very orthodox. They detest such visits.

Let me tell you that I highly appreciate your desire to help me in my studies. I shall certainly accept your help as and when necessary.

I am inclined to be better acquainted with you. But I cannot say that I love you.

I am yet too young to understand the various aspects of a love-affair.

Right now I feel a little confused. Please do not take offence at what I am saying. I do not want to offend or displease you. Try to understand my limitations.

Yours sincerely,

Bina

(Full name and address of the recipient)

98. A passionate love letter from a lover to his beloved

(Full address of the writer, and date)

Dearest Anuradha,

I saw you in the college library last Monday. My heart has since been crying for you day and night. Please take me at my word when I say that I cannot think of life without you. It is nothing but a simple and pure truth. There is no exaggeration about it even in the least. You are out of sight, but you are in front of the eyes of my mind every moment. You are certainly a sparkling spot on my vision. To speak the truth, I am extremely lucky that you have so kindly encouraged me to love you from the core of my heart. None can deny the fact that you are great and grand. You are a real beauty in the true sense of the term. I am most glad that God, the Greatest, has benignly endowed you with all the qualities of head and heart. Even a prince will surely fall in love with you at the first sight.

He will gladly, solemnly, respectfully and humbly stoop to woo and love you. Anuradha, I have wholly lost my heart to you.

But in return, I have found heaven and refuge (shelter/protection) in you.

I swear by almighty God that I love you most deeply and sincerely. I shall never do anything to hurt your feelings. The fact that you also love me, is a great spur to my present hard work and future achievements. It has added a new dimension to my life. Your true love will always inspire me in every field of my various activities.

I hope this finds you in the best of spirits.

With deepest love and best wishes,

Yours for ever,

Dharam Pal

(Full name and address of the recipient)

99. Love letter from a girl to her would-be husband

(Full address of the writer, and date)

Dearest Ravi,

I have just received your lovely letter. The contents of the letter have actually filled my heart with great delight. In other words, I am beside myself with joy. I do not find adequate words in language to express the depth of my delight. Please keep on writing such wonderful letters to me as often as you can. It is really a matter of tremendous joy to know that your parents have approved and confirmed our engagement. I am the happiest girl in the world. After we get married, the days, months and years will be splendid. We shall think, plan, work and enjoy together.

The happy news has excited me so much that I can hardly keep my pen steady. You can very well imagine the over-happy frame of my mind. My heart is throbbing fast with the excitement caused by the happy news. I have all these days been talking to my sisters-in-law and friends about your brilliant academic achievements, your handsome looks, and your deep love for me. You will certainly be very glad to know that I never feel tired of telling even my mother what you mean to me. She patiently listens to me, and takes great delight in it.

With most profound love and best wishes,

Yours,

Rohini

(Full name and address of the recipient)

100. Love letter from a male teacher to one of his girl students in a school

(Full address of the writer, and date)

My dear Sundari,

At the outset, let me tell you frankly that I love you very deeply. I am very much smitten by the joy of desire to possess you. I always think of you. The other day I wanted to talk to you on this subject, but I could not muster enough courage to do so. Now I am making an open confession of it to you. I strongly feel that you also have love for me. Your suggestive smiles and gestures also confirm that you love me. Had you not shown signs of your love for me like this, I would not have written this confessional letter to you.

Know it for certain that your enticing ways and stunning

physical beauty sharpen my love for you all the more. Darling, I must tell you frankly about my intense passion for you and you alone. You are the only girl for me. My passionate love for you has become a matter of life and death for me.

Let me tell you how I shall love you. I shall sit beside you. I shall go on staring at you every moment till I fall asleep at night or day. This is the way I shall love you for ever. I shall never do anything to lower your dignity or to damage your reputation as a girl of good character in the estimation of the public. This is the way I shall love you.

Sundari, you are intelligent, mature, attractive, polite, and amiable by nature. You can very well understand my helplessness. I am sure you will never disappoint me. On my part, I assure you that I shall do my best to make you happy and cheerful till the last moment of my life.

Will you very kindly take the trouble to send me a line in reply as soon as possible ?

I hope this finds you all at home in the best of health and happiness.

With deepest love and best wishes,

Yours for ever,

Himadri

(Full name and address of the recipient)